SEQUENTIAL WORDS
with Your Pets

By Kristen Rajczak

Gareth Stevens
Publishing

Please visit our website, www.garethstevens.com. For a free color catalog of all our high-quality books, call toll free 1-800-542-2595 or fax 1-877-542-2596.

Library of Congress Cataloging-in-Publication Data

Rajczak, Kristen.
Sequential words with your pets / by Kristen Rajczak.
   p. cm. — (Write right)
Includes index.
ISBN 978-1-4339-9078-6 (pbk.)
ISBN 978-1-4339-9079-3 (6-pack)
ISBN 978-1-4339-9077-9 (library binding)
1. English language—Sentences—Juvenile literature. 2. English language—Grammar—Juvenile literature.
3. Pets—Juvenile literature. I. Rajczak, Kristen. II. Title.
PE1441.R35 2014
428.2—d23

First Edition

Published in 2014 by
Gareth Stevens Publishing
111 East 14th Street, Suite 349
New York, NY 10003

Designer: Sarah Liddell
Editor: Kristen Rajczak

Photo credits: Cover, p. 1 Comstock/Thinkstock.com; p. 5 Steve Lyne/Dorling Kindersley/Getty Images; p. 7 Nick Dolding/Photodisc/Getty Images; p. 9 © iStockphoto.com/sonyae; p. 11 Dorling Kindersley/ Dorling Kindersley/Getty Images; p. 13 Daniel Laflor/the Agency Collection/Getty Images; p. 15 Chris Bernard/E+/Getty Images; p. 17 Ron Levine/Digital Vision/Getty Images; p. 19 Steve Shott/ Dorling Kindersley/Getty Images.

Printed in the United States of America

CPSIA compliance information: Batch #CS13GS: For further information contact Gareth Stevens, New York, New York at 1-800-542-2595.

CONTENTS

Words in the glossary appear in **bold** type the first time they are used in the text.

TRANSITION BASICS

A transition is a word or **phrase** that helps bring two ideas together. Using transitions makes a piece of writing clearer because these words act as clues to the reader about what's coming next. Some transition words like *also, additionally*, and *furthermore* let the reader know information will be added. *For example, that is*, and *in other words* **signal** to the reader that a point will be made clearer.

Sequential words are another kind of transition. They tell the reader in what order events happen.

ON THE WRITE TRACK

Transitions don't have to be used with every sentence. They usually come between paragraphs to move from one idea to another.

Many pet owners use hand signals to tell their pet to sit or stay. Writers use transition words to signal to readers to stop or keep reading!

5

JUST IN TIME!

Sequential words are used to show chronological, or time, order. They're especially helpful when telling a story.

Mimi and her brother wanted to buy a fish tank for their fish. **First**, they had to get their parents' permission. **Then**, they had to find out how much the tank cost. **Lastly**, they had to save the money to buy the tank.

The highlighted words in the example above are just a few sequential words. Read on to learn more!

ON THE WRITE TRACK

The word "sequential" comes from the word "sequence." A sequence is an order of events or things. For example, "1, 2, 3, 4" is a sequence of numbers.

NUMBER ORDER

Some of the most commonly used sequential words are **numerical**, such as first, second, and third. At the start, to begin with, next, and after are all sequential transitions that can put events in order, too.

Davis was in charge of taking care of the family dog, Jelly, every morning. **First**, he clipped on Jelly's **leash**. **Then**, he and Jelly walked around the block. **After the walk**, Davis let Jelly off the leash and filled her bowl with food.

ON THE WRITE TRACK

Today, tomorrow, and yesterday can all be used as sequential words. They show time!

Numerical words are often used to explain a **routine**, such as Davis walking and feeding the dog each morning.

9

ALL AT ONCE

What if you want to write about two **concurrent** events? You can use sequential words for that, too! Transition terms that signal concurrent events include **at the same time** and **meanwhile**.

Abed put his gerbil in its exercise ball so it could move around the room. **At the same time**, his sister cleaned the gerbil's cage.

Hannah was playing with her new kitten in her bedroom. **Meanwhile**, the family's older cat, Gus, scratched at her door. He wanted to play, too!

ON THE WRITE TRACK

Some sequential words show digression, or a sudden change of subject. By the way and to change the topic are phrases that would introduce a digression.

Starting a sentence with **while** is also a way to show concurrence: **While** Hannah played with her new kitten, the family's older cat scratched at the door.

CONTINUING THE FUN

Sequential words can be used to show that an action has continued or that some time has passed between one event and the next.

Afterward lets the reader know one action is over and another is about to begin.

Arnie let his pet spider out of its tank while he did his homework. But **afterward**, he couldn't find it!

Eventually and **finally** signal that a good deal of time passed before the next action occurred.

Micah's puppy chewed a hole through his shoe! **Eventually**, Micah found the chewed-up shoe and was angry it was ruined.

ON THE WRITE TRACK

After a digression, sequential words can show a return to the original topic. Anyway, to get back to the point, and at any rate can all be used for this.

Without words that show time has passed, a story could be pretty boring!

13

END IT ON THIS

It's important for a writer to signal to the reader that a piece of writing is nearing its end. Use sequential words such as **in the end**, **lastly**, **at last**, and **to conclude**.

Sweetie the **Great Dane** had lived with the Young family since soon after she was born. At first, she wasn't much bigger than a basketball. When she was 1 year old, Sweetie was too big for her favorite chair! **At last**, Sweetie stopped growing. She weighed more than 120 pounds (54 kg)!

ON THE WRITE TRACK

Sequential words of **summation** also may signal the end of a topic or a piece or writing. Thus, altogether, overall, and in summary are just some of these.

Words of conclusion and summation can help make an argument more effective.

15

WHICH WAY?

Sequential words are used not only when telling a story, but also when giving directions.

Here's some advice about choosing the right pet!

At the start, make a list of some cool pets. **Then**, remove the pets that have needs you can't fulfill easily. If you don't have lots of land, a horse wouldn't be happy! **Next**, decide how much money you can spend on the pet. Fish tanks can be pricey! **Finally**, ask your parents their opinion.

ON THE WRITE TRACK

Teaching someone to do something is another way you might give directions. Do you want to teach your sister how to clean out your mouse's cage? You'll need to use sequential words.

Whether you want to help someone find your house or tell them how to make a sandwich, numerical, summation, and ending words are needed.

NOTE THE CHANGES

Since pets don't talk, it's hard to tell if they get sick. You have to pay close attention and notice changes in their habits. At the **vet's** office, you'll need to use sequential words to tell about the changes you observed.

Leonard was worried about his rabbit, Jasper. He told the vet:

"**Yesterday**, Jasper wouldn't eat. He usually eats really fast! **Anyway**, **then** I saw his eyes were all red. **After a while**, he let me look closer, but I didn't know how to help him."

ON THE WRITE TRACK

In some science projects, the changes that occur can tell a lot about the project's topic. Sequential words are often used in scientific writing to give a clear order to the events leading up to and following a major change.

Leonard was right to take Jasper to the vet when he thought the rabbit's eyes were bothering him. Using sequential words can help the vet figure out when the problem started and how long it's been going on.

ORDER, PLEASE

See the many ways to use sequential words as transitions below.

Before today, Bettina had never owned a bird. **At first**, she was nervous. What if he didn't like his cage? **After** he was in it, though, he happily flew around. **Meanwhile**, Bettina tried to name him. **Then**, her bird made a sound—chirp! It seemed like the perfect name.

Later, Bettina opened the cage—and Chirp flew out! She **finally** used some food to get him back inside. **All in all**, it was a great day!

ON THE WRITE TRACK

A comma often follows sequential words and phrases, especially if they start a **dependent clause**.

WHEN TO USE SEQUENTIAL WORDS

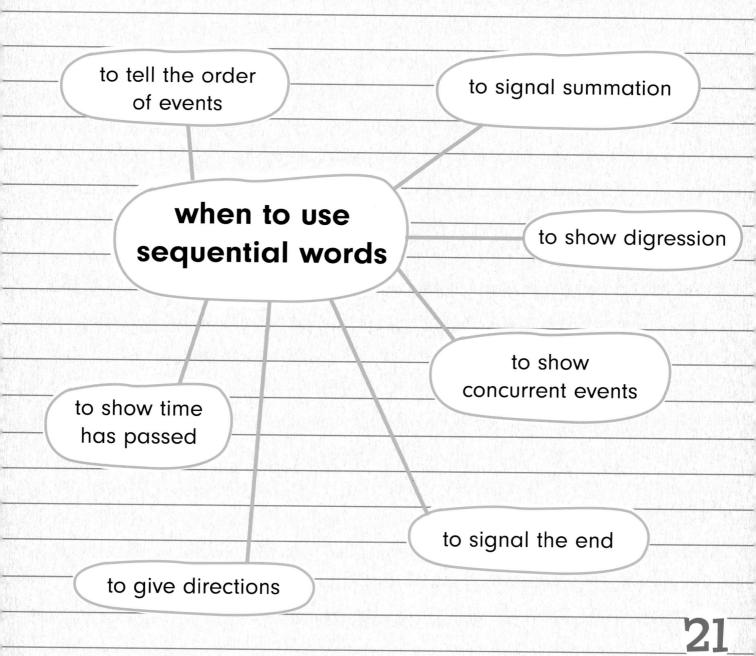

to tell the order of events

to signal summation

when to use sequential words

to show digression

to show time has passed

to show concurrent events

to give directions

to signal the end

GLOSSARY

concurrent: occurring at the same time

dependent clause: a group of words that has a subject and verb but cannot stand on its own as a sentence

Great Dane: a kind of dog that grows to be very large

leash: a long band used to lead an animal

numerical: having to do with numbers

phrase: a group of words

routine: the usual course of events

signal: a sign or action that lets someone know something

summation: a review of points made in a piece of writing

vet: a doctor who takes care of animals

FOR MORE INFORMATION

BOOKS

Fogarty, Mignon. *Grammar Girl Presents the Ultimate Writing Guide for Students*. New York, NY: Henry Holt and Co., 2011.

Ganeri, Anita. *Stories*. Chicago, IL: Heinemann Library, 2013.

WEBSITES

Fun Grammar Games for Kids
www.funenglishgames.com/grammargames.html
Practice lots of good writing skills on this interactive, free website.

Transition Words
jc-schools.net/write/transition.htm
Use this list to learn more transition words and when to use them.

INDEX